THE UNIVERSE

EXPLORING THE UNIVERSE

NEIL ARDLEY

Editorial planning
Philip Steele

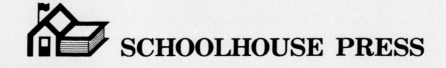

SCHOOLHOUSE PRESS

Copyright © 1988 by Schoolhouse Press, Inc.
191 Spring Street, Lexington,
Massachussetts 02173-8087
ISBN 0-8086-1126-7 (hardback)
ISBN 0-8086-1133-X (paperback)

Original copyright, © Macmillan Education Limited 1987
© BLA Publishing Limited 1987

Designed and produced by BLA Publishing Limited,
East Grinstead, Sussex, England.

Also in LONDON · HONG KONG · TAIPEI · SINGAPORE · NEW YORK

A Ling Kee Company

Illustrations by Sallie Alane Reason, Val Sangster/Linden
Artists, Brian Watson/Linden Artists, Steve Weston/Linden
Artists
Color origination by Reprocraft Studios
Printed in Hong Kong

88/89/90/91   6 5 4 3 2 1

Photographic credits

t = top b = bottom l = left r = right

cover: Science Photo Library

7*t* ZEFA; 7*b*, 9 Michael Holford; 10*t* Science Photo
Library; 10*b* Ann Ronan Picture Library; 11, 12/13, 15
Science Photo Library; 17 John Mason; 19*t*, 19*b* Science
Photo Library; 20*t*, 20*b* Royal Observatory, Edinburgh;
21, 22, 23*t*, 23*b*, 25*t*, 25*b*, 26 Science Photo Library;
27*t* Kobol Collection; 28*t*, 28*b*, 31*t*, 31*b*, 32, 38, 39*t*, 39*b*
Science Photo Library; 41 Mansell Collection; 42, 45
Science Photo Library

Note to the reader
In this book there are some words in the text which are printed in **bold** type. This shows that the word is listed in the glossary on page 46. The glossary gives a brief explanation of words which may be new to you.

Contents

Introduction

The **universe** is everything that exists. It includes our **planet** earth with all its living things. It includes the **moon** which travels around the earth. The universe also includes the **sun**. The sun is a great ball of hot **gases**.

A total of nine planets circles the sun. Some of them, like Saturn, have their own moons. The sun and its planets are called the **solar system**. The solar system is very big, but it is only a tiny part of the universe.

Beyond the Solar System

Every **star** you see in the sky is another sun. There are millions and millions of stars. **Telescopes** help us to see stars which are too faint to be seen with the eyes. Many stars must have their own planets and moons, but these are too far away to be seen even with a telescope.

How big is the universe? No one knows the answer. We cannot see the edges of the universe. Perhaps, they are too far away. Perhaps, the universe has no edges and goes on forever. This is a puzzle we still have to solve.

▼ An astronaut floats in space high above the earth. A line links him to his spacecraft. The astronaut can look out at the universe with its millions of stars.

Finding Out about the Universe

In between the stars and planets, there is empty **space**. There are streaks of gas and tiny specks of **dust**, but no air for us to breathe. When people travel in space, they must take their own supply of air with them.

Can you think what it would be like to travel in space around the earth? You could see our planet with its blue seas and white clouds. You could see the moon catching the light of the sun. The deep black of outer space would be dotted with stars.

The universe would seem to stretch out forever, and you would soon see how tiny our world really is.

People have tried to find out about the universe for thousands of years. In this book, we shall look at some of the ways in which this can be done. We shall look at telescopes and other things we can use to map out the universe. We shall look at ways in which people and machines can be sent into space. We shall learn how much people have found out so far and what ideas they have about the universe.

Gods and Stars

▲ A priestess worships the moon goddess during the Stone Age. Long ago, people knew little about the sun, the moon, and the stars. They thought they must be gods or goddesses.

When people first looked up into the sky, they saw that the sun gave them light and warmth during the day. The moon gave them light at night when it was dark. Some people thought that the sun was a god who lived in the sky and that the moon was a goddess. People worshipped the sun and the moon. These people hoped to please their gods, so they would always bring light and warmth.

People believed that many gods lived in the sky. For example, the planet Mars is named after the Roman god of war. The Romans could see that the planet's light was red like blood. We still use many Roman names for the stars and the planets.

Who Made the Universe?

Long ago, people knew very little about the universe. They could see the land and the sea, and many people thought that the world must be flat. They could see the sun, the moon, and the stars. They asked themselves how the universe had begun. They thought of ways in which they could explain it all. All over the world, there are old stories about how the universe was first made.

The Norse people, who live in northern Europe, used to tell this story about the making of the universe: At first, there was nothing at all. Then, clouds, ice, and fire began to form. As the ice melted, a wicked giant called Ymir appeared. A huge cow also came out of the ice. As the cow licked the ice, the first human being called Buri came out.

His three grandsons were gods, and they killed the giant Ymir. They made the earth, the seas, and the sky from the giant's body. Sparks from fires rose into the new sky, and these became the sun, the moon, and the stars.

Stargazers

People noticed how the sun, the moon, and the stars seemed to move through the sky. They measured the passing of time by noting how long these movements took. In Egypt, people made **calendars** with days, months, and years. They worked out the best date to sow their crops each year. This helped them to make sure that the harvest would be a good one.

▲ This circle of stones, called Stonehenge, was built about 4,000 years ago in the south of England. People may have used it to watch the sky. The sun, the moon, and the stars seem to touch some of the stones at certain times of the year.

▼ This picture was drawn in Egypt about 3,000 years ago. It shows the sun god, Ra. Ra was lord of the whole sky. People and animals were thought to have been made from Ra's tears.

The First Sky Maps

The more people looked up at the night sky, the more they wondered how the sun, the moon, and the stars moved. Some people began to measure the movements with great care. They were the first **astronomers**. Astronomers are people who study the sky.

▼ The first great astronomers lived in Greece. One of them was called Hipparchus. He lived over 2,000 years ago. He made a map of the sky showing a thousand stars. He was the first person to work out the distance of the moon from the earth.

The First Astronomers

The first stargazers saw that the stars always stayed the same distance from each other. But they also noticed that there were five points of light which did not seem to stay in the same place. They seemed to wander among the stars. These were planets.

Astronomers tried to explain how all these movements were taking place. They tried to explain how the universe worked. The first ideas came from Greece about 2,500 years ago. The Greeks thought that the earth was round and was at the center of the universe. They thought that the moon, the sun, and the planets moved around the earth. They thought that all the stars moved at the same speed and were far away.

8

Groups of Stars

None of the first astronomers had telescopes. They were not used until much later. People had to rely on their own eyes and on simple tools, or **instruments**. Some of these were **sundials**. Sundials use a shadow cast by the sun to show the time of day. Other instruments were used to measure where the sun, the moon, the planets, or the stars appeared in the sky. Some of them were very large.

Astronomers also made maps of the sky which showed where all the stars were. These maps showed the patterns the stars seemed to make when viewed from the earth. Each group of stars is called a **constellation**.

◄ The astrolabe was invented by the Arabs. It was used to check where the stars were in the sky. The person looked along the pointer and turned it so that it pointed towards a star. The instrument then showed the height of that star in the sky.

▶ The astronomer Ptolemy lived in Egypt nearly 1,900 years ago. He wrote a famous book called *Almagest*. In it, he said that the sun, the moon, and the planets all move around the earth.

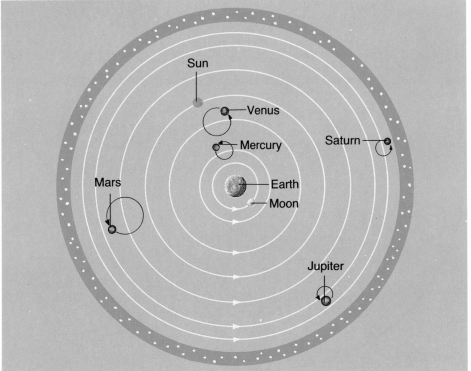

Sun
Venus
Mercury
Saturn
Mars
Earth
Moon
Jupiter

The New Science

Most people continued to believe the Greek idea of the universe for more than a thousand years. It was wrong. The earth is not at the center of the universe. Our world moves around the sun as the other planets do also. Only the moon moves around the earth. The stars lie far away in space.

One Greek astronomer, named Aristarchus, had thought of this idea nearly 1,250 years ago. It explained the way the planets appear to move in the sky. No one agreed with him. They could not believe that something as big as the earth could move.

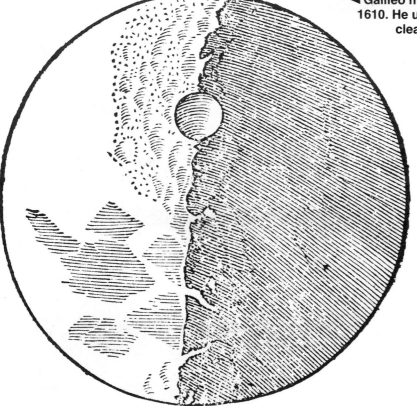

◀ Galileo made this drawing of the moon in 1610. He used a telescope, and his picture clearly shows the big craters on the moon. It was the first picture to show people what other worlds out in space really look like. Not everyone believed it was true. Some people thought that the images seen in telescopes were ghosts!

◀ Nicolaus Copernicus became a doctor, but his main interest was astronomy. He watched the planets and calculated that they moved around the sun. So many people disagreed with him that he did not dare publish his ideas until just before his death.

▶ The astronomer Halley was a friend of Isaac Newton. Halley worked out that this same ball of gas and dust had been seen in 1531, 1607, and 1682. He said it would appear again in 1758. When it did, sixteen years after his death, it was called Halley's comet, in his honor.

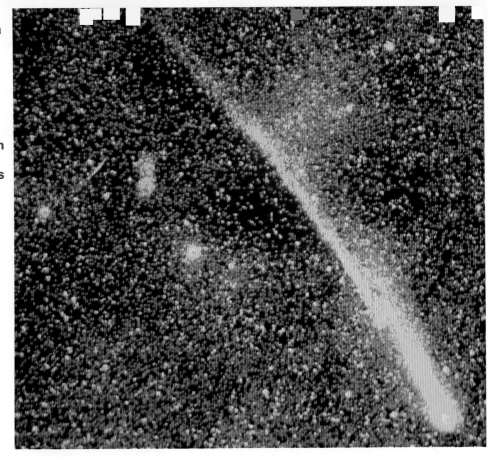

Finding Out the Truth

In 1543, Nicolaus Copernicus, a Polish astronomer, said that the earth must move around the sun. Most people still did not agree. Then, in 1609, an Italian called Galileo Galilei used one of the first telescopes to look at the sky. He saw that Copernicus was right.

Astronomy became a new science. At last, astronomers could look out into the universe and see what was there. Since then, three more planets and many more stars have been found. Vast groups of stars called **galaxies** and clouds of gas and dust could be seen.

Movements in Space

People were now sure that the planets move around the sun. They still did not know why. A German astronomer named Johann Kepler worked for many years to find out how the planets moved. He studied their paths, or **orbits**, around the sun. In 1609, he proved that the orbits were egg-shaped, or **elliptical**.

In 1687, the English scientist Isaac Newton said that a pulling force called **gravity** makes things fall. Anything thrown into the air is pulled back down to the earth's surface. The same force holds the planets in orbit around the sun and the moon in orbit around the earth.

The new science of astronomy soon showed that the solar system is not the most important part of the universe. The sun is just one of millions of stars in our galaxy. There are many other galaxies far away in space.

Finding Out about Space

In the last hundred years, we have found out more and more about the universe. We now know that it is very big and that there are millions of galaxies which are moving through space. We have found out about the large glowing clouds of gas and dust, which are called **nebulae**.

The Facts So Far

The more we find out about the universe, the more puzzling it becomes. Many things in space are too far away for us to see. They are beyond the reach of any **spacecraft** that has been made. How much do we know?

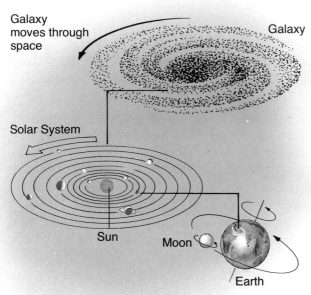

▲ The moon moves around the earth, while the earth moves around the sun. The sun, too, spins around and moves with the whole galaxy as it wheels around through space. Nothing in the universe is still. We often talk about the speed of objects in space. What we mean is how fast that object is moving towards, away from, or around something else.

Galaxies

★ Our galaxy is called the Milky Way. It contains about 100,000,000,000 stars. The sun is just one of them. Our solar system is moving around the galaxy at a speed of 505,000 miles per hour.

★ Our galaxy is one of a group of about thirty galaxies. Groups like this are called galaxy **clusters**. Our cluster is known as the Local Group.

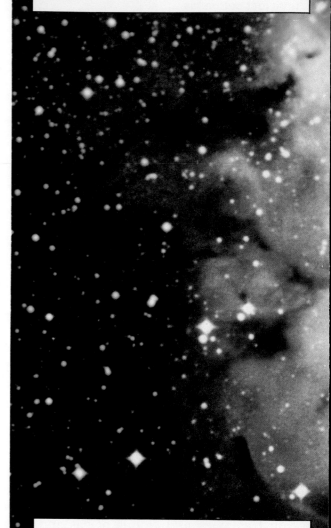

▲ The Trifid nebula is a vast glowing cloud far away in the galaxy. It is made up of gas and dust. Its light takes about 6,500 years to reach us across space. We say that it is about 6,500 "light years" away.

Comets

★ A **comet** is a ball of dust and frozen gas. It orbits the sun. When a comet comes close to the sun, some of the frozen gas melts and streams out behind the comet like a long tail.

★ Halley's comet is one of the most famous comets. It takes seventy-six years to orbit the sun. Halley's comet can be seen in pictures which are hundreds of years old. Its last visit was in 1986.

★ A large cloud of comets lies at the edge of the solar system and far beyond the planet Pluto. The cloud might contain millions of comets. The comets orbit the sun.

The Solar System

★ We know that there are nine planets in orbit around the sun. There might be a tenth planet, but it has not been found yet.

★ The solar system is about four and a half billion years old. It was formed from a cloud of gas and dust floating in space.

★ The planet Mercury is the fastest moving planet. It moves around the sun at a speed of 108,000 miles per hour.

Strange Discoveries

★ A **pulsar** is a star that can spin very fast. As it spins, it sends out a beam of energy. The energy seems to turn on and off, or pulse.

★ A **black hole** sucks in everything near it. It is a part of space with very strong gravity. The pulling force is so strong that even light is pulled back into the hole. That is why it looks black.

★ **Quasars** look like stars, but they give out a much greater amount of energy. No one really knows what they are. They might be distant galaxies disappearing into a black hole inside them.

Light and Other Rays

On a clear night, you can see lots of stars. You see the stars because they send out rays of light. The light moves at a speed of 186,000 miles per second. The stars are so far away that it takes years for their light to travel through space. At last, the rays reach the earth. They pass through the layer of gases that we call the air, or **atmosphere**.

Types of Ray

We can see rays of light from the earth. There are many other kinds of rays in space that we cannot see. They are also given off by stars, planets, galaxies, and nebulae. Most of these rays, like light, travel with a wavy motion. We measure them by the distance from one crest to another. This is called a **wavelength**.

Rays which have the shortest wavelengths of all are called **gamma rays**. **X-rays** have very short wavelengths. **Ultraviolet** rays have a longer wavelength, but are still shorter than light. Rays which have wavelengths slightly longer than light are called **infrared** rays. The longest wavelengths of all are known as **radio waves**.

▼ Light travels in waves. We see different wavelengths of light as different colors. The only difference between light and other rays, such as radio waves or X-rays, is the wavelength.

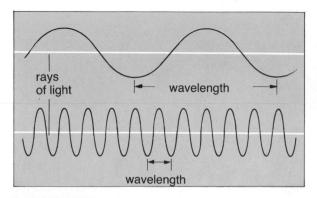

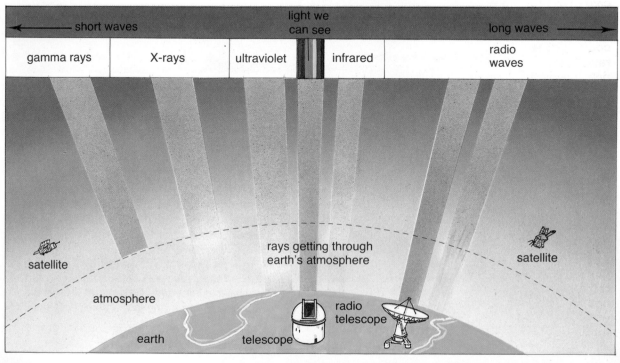

Not all kinds of rays travel with a wavy motion. Some are made up of tiny pieces of matter called **particles**. They stream through space at very high speeds. They are called **cosmic rays**. The sun gives out bursts of cosmic rays, as do stars when they explode.

Picking Up the Rays

All kinds of instruments are used to pick up rays from space. **Optical telescopes** gather light rays. They can show us a distant planet and make it look nearer. **Radio telescopes** pick up radio waves coming from objects in space. Computers can turn the waves into pictures we can see.

X-rays and gamma rays cannot pass through the dust and gases of the earth's atmosphere. Many infrared and ultraviolet rays are also blocked. We can get around this problem by sending instruments into space. These instruments can pick up the rays in space and then send signals back to the earth.

We cannot visit stars or distant galaxies. The only way we can find out about them is to study the rays they give off. Rays can tell us how far away objects are and what they are made of. Rays can show us objects which we cannot see with our eyes. Rays can pass through dense clouds of dust and nebulae. We can use them to find out more about the universe.

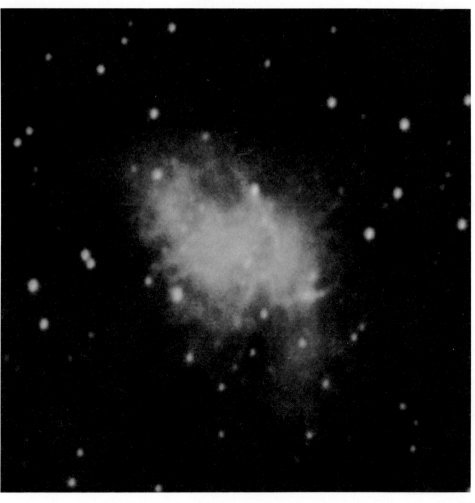

▶ The Crab nebula can be seen through a telescope. It is the remains of a star that has exploded. It is a cloud of gas which looks like a crab. We can see the light it gives out. We cannot see the many other rays which come from it. If we could see gamma rays, the Crab nebula would be one of the brightest objects in the sky.

◀ Rays of all wavelengths travel through space and strike the earth's atmosphere. The complete range goes from the very short gamma rays to long radio waves. Only light rays and radio waves can pass through the atmosphere.

Optical Telescopes

To look far out into space, you need a telescope. **Binoculars** will help you to see some objects, such as the moon, much more clearly. But it is hard to hold them still long enough to study objects in the sky. It is better to use a telescope. This can be attached to a tripod so that you do not need to hold it.
Never look at the sun through binoculars or a telescope. If you do, you will badly damage your eyes.

How Telescopes Work

There are two kinds of optical telescope. They both work in much the same way. They pick up light rays coming from an object, such as the moon. Then, these telescopes make the light rays meet inside the tube. A picture, or image, of the object is formed.

In a **refracting telescope**, the light rays are bent to make them meet inside. They are bent when the rays pass through a big **lens** at the front of the telescope. **Reflecting telescopes** have a curved mirror inside of them. The mirror **reflects** the rays, so that they meet. The wider a telescope is, the better it works. This is because it picks up more light.

The astronomer first looks through the small telescope on top in order to find the right group of stars. Then, the astronomer moves the whole telescope to bring just one into view.

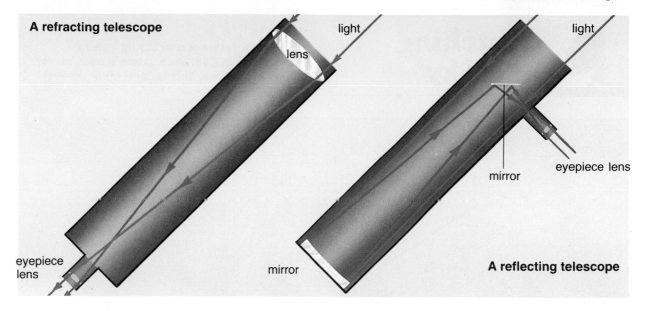

A refracting telescope

light

lens

light

eyepiece lens

mirror

eyepiece
lens

mirror

A reflecting telescope

▲ In a refracting telescope, the light rays pass through a glass lens. This bends them so that they meet and form an image. The eyepiece lens passes this image into the eye. A reflecting telescope uses mirrors. These mirrors reflect the light rays to form an image which is seen through the eyepiece lens.

▼ The biggest refracting telescope in the world is at Yerkes Observatory near Chicago. It was built in 1897. Its lens is forty inches across. Very large lenses do not give very clear images. The biggest telescopes built today all use mirrors instead.

Using a Telescope

Watching a star or taking a photograph through the telescope can take a long time. The telescope will soon start to point away from the object which the astronomer is looking at because the earth is always turning. To solve this problem, telescopes may be turned by a small motor. This keeps the telescope pointing at the object. In some places, the whole building in which the telescope is kept can turn as well.

Giant Telescopes

Some reflecting telescopes are very big. The largest one in the world is in the USSR. The mirror is nineteen feet across and weighs seventy-seven tons. In some telescopes, a large number of smaller mirrors are used to gather light instead of one large one.

Watching the Sky

▼ The Hale Telescope at Mount Palomar Observatory in California. It has a main mirror 200 inches across, and several other smaller mirrors.

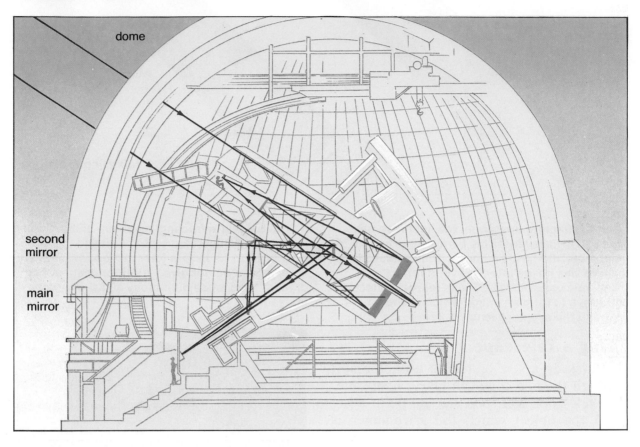

dome

second mirror

main mirror

Astronomers work in **observatories**. These large buildings contain telescopes and the other equipment needed for watching the stars. The telescopes are kept under curved roofs called **domes**. The dome opens so that the telescope can look out at the night sky.

Most observatories are at the tops of high mountains and in places where the weather is dry. This is because the air is very clear there. People can get a good view of the stars. In other places, dust and clouds in the air spoil the view. The observatory must also be far away from the glaring lights of cities and towns.

Observatories have been built all over the world, so people can view all parts of the sky. There are observatory sites in California, Arizona, and Hawaii in the USA. Other important sites are in the southern part of the USSR, Chile in South America, Australia, and the Canary Islands in the North Atlantic Ocean.

A Day's Work

Many different kinds of work are done in observatories. Some people may be looking at stars. Other people may be studying comets or looking for objects like pulsars and quasars.

Often, there are different kinds of telescope in the same place. They can be used to carry out a number of tasks. Some observatories use a special telescope to study the sun. Some use **Schmidt telescopes**. Schmidt telescopes are able to take pictures of large parts of the sky instead of just single stars. This means that the whole sky can be mapped in better detail than before. They can also show us faint stars not seen before.

In the old days, astronomers had to spend hours peering through the eyepiece of a telescope. Today, the image is often picked up by an **electronic** device which reacts to light. It can see better than the human eye. It can find very faint objects and show them on a screen.

Working Together

The big observatories cost a lot of money to build and to run. They are often owned by countries or by universities. People from different countries often work with each other. They share the costs. They tell each other what they have found out.

▲ The largest telescope at the Kitt Peak Observatory is under the dome. It has a mirror 157 inches across. You can see how big the telescope is compared to the person working near the center.

▶ This is Kitt Peak Observatory in Arizona. It has fourteen telescopes. This is more than any other observatory in the world has.

19

Getting the Picture

The pictures of space we get today are very clear. They can show distant stars and glowing clouds of gas in great detail. Today, we have very good cameras. We also have other devices we can attach to telescopes. They can record the image of the object we are looking at. They can measure the light rays. They help us find out more about the universe.

▶ The Great Nebula in Orion. This picture was taken with a Schmidt telescope, like the one shown below.

◀ The Anglo-Australian observatory is on Siding Spring mountain in New South Wales, Australia. It has a thirteen foot reflecting telescope and a four foot Schmidt telescope. The Schmidt telescope is very good for taking pictures of wide areas of the night sky.

▶ Each of these patterns of color shows the spectrum of a star. Each spectrum has colored bands and dark lines. The bands and lines are different in each spectrum. Astronomers measure the width of the bands and lines and the distance between them.

The bands of colors are made by the hot gases in the star. The dark lines are made by the cooler gases around the star. Different gases give different bands and lines. The position of the bands shows how fast the star is moving.

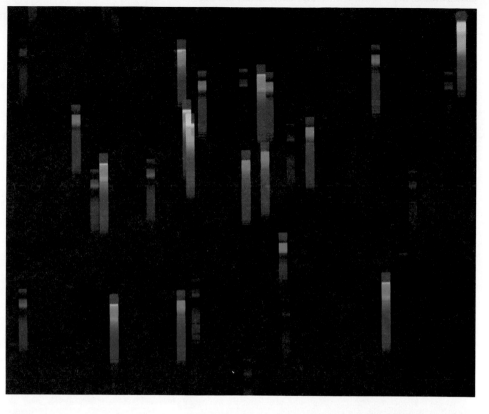

Cameras and Light

Special cameras are used to take pictures of the night sky. Their film must be able to pick up very faint sources of light. Colored **filters** are often used when the picture is taken. Filters stop light of a certain color from getting through. This makes other colors stronger. It helps some stars to appear very clearly.

Many objects are too faint to appear even if a camera is used. In this case, a special device called a **photon counter** is attached to the telescope. This picks up tiny amounts of light. It can make the image of a star 10 million times brighter than it first appears. Very faint objects can then be seen and photographed.

Working with Light Rays

Astronomers do not only take pictures of the images seen in the telescope. They also take pictures of the complete range, or **spectrum**, of light rays. When light from the sun passes through a raindrop, it is bent. We see the colors of the spectrum as a rainbow.

The same thing happens if light passes through a piece of glass shaped like a triangle. This piece of glass is called a **prism**. A machine called a **spectrograph** uses a prism to measure the spectrum of light given out by stars. It can tell us what a star is made of. It can tell us how hot it is. It can also show how fast objects are moving through space.

How are the sizes of stars measured? Astronomers use a special device called an **interferometer**. It is like a pair of telescopes which combine two or more pictures of a star. Scientists measure the shapes made by the light. This tells them how big the star is. The best interferometer is in Australia. It could measure the width of a human hair sixty miles away!

Computers and Colors

The biggest telescopes today are controlled by computers. The computers can move the telescopes and the mirrors inside them. Computers are also used to make the pictures better if they are not clear. They can change a picture to show any details. Computers can store facts and figures. They can work out math problems. They save us a lot of hard work.

Instant Pictures

There are tiny pieces of a substance called **silicon** inside computers. The pieces carry **electricity**. We call them **microchips**.

A special kind of microchip is used in video cameras. It is also used to take pictures of space. The image of a star falls on the microchip. On the surface of the chip are rows of tiny spots. They react to light. The microchip changes the image into electronic signals. These are stored in a computer. They can show the image in color on a screen at any time.

Color Coding

Look at a photograph of a galaxy. Your eyes are telling you what it looks like, but they cannot see everything. The picture might show just the bright center of the galaxy. It might miss the outer clouds of faint stars. We could take a photograph to show the faintest parts of the galaxy. Then, other faint stars would appear in the photograph as well. They would get in the way of the galaxy.

◀ This is a microchip taken from a camera inside a telescope. The chip is covered with up to a million tiny spots. When light falls on the chip, the rows of spots send electronic signals to a computer. The computer turns the signals into a picture on a television screen.

▲ The Andromeda galaxy is more than two million light years away. It is the same shape as our own galaxy, but is about twice as large. This photograph was taken through a telescope, and it shows us what the galaxy actually looks like.

► This photograph was taken with the radio waves coming from the Andromeda galaxy. A computer has been used to give different parts of the picture different colors. The parts of the galaxy coming towards us are blue. The parts moving away are orange.

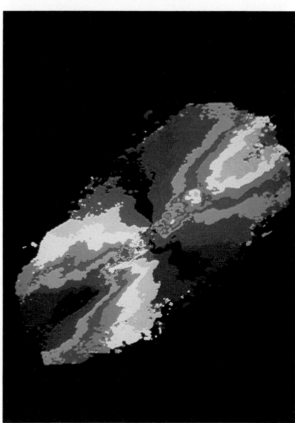

The computer can solve this problem. It can take the image of the galaxy and make it clearer for us. It can take away any stars that we do not want to see. It can color in different parts of the galaxy. The bright center can be given one color. The fainter parts can be given other colors. This makes it easy for us to tell each part of the galaxy from the other parts. The colors used are not the real colors. This kind of picture is called a **false-color image**.

Radio Telescopes

Radio telescopes can pick up radio waves from the most distant parts of the universe. They look like huge bowls which point up to the sky. Radio telescopes do not look like the big reflecting telescopes, but they work in much the same way.

Radio waves come from all kinds of objects in space. They come from the sun, the planets, the stars, and the galaxies. The bowl-shaped **radio dish** acts like a curved mirror. It reflects the waves inwards. They meet above the center of the dish. There, an **antenna** picks up the radio waves. It turns them into electrical signals.

These signals then go into a computer. They can be used to make maps and pictures of the objects in space. The false-color picture of the Andromeda galaxy on page 23 was made with a radio telescope.

Pointing the Telescopes

Radio telescopes can pick up radio waves during the day as well as during the night. Often, they have dishes which can be moved. The dish can be pointed towards any part of the sky. The biggest dish of this kind is in Effelsberg, West Germany. It is 330 feet across.

▼ Many radio telescopes have a dish which can be turned to follow a star or a galaxy as the earth spins. It can pick up radio waves coming from objects in space. The largest dish like this is 330 feet across.

antenna

dish reflects waves to center

radio telescope

► The largest single radio telescope in the world is at Arecibo in Puerto Rico. The dish is built into a valley. It cannot be moved. It picks up radio waves from objects as they move across the sky.

▼ The Very Large Array is in the deserts of the state of New Mexico. It is a group of twenty-seven radio telescopes. The telescopes can be moved along railroad tracks. There are three tracks shaped like a Y. Each arm of the Y is thirteen miles long.

Some radio telescopes have dishes which cannot be moved. They point to the part of the sky that passes over them as the earth spins. The biggest radio telescope of this kind is the Arecibo dish on the island of Puerto Rico. It is 990 feet across.

Groups of Telescopes

The dish of a radio telescope has to be very big. This helps it to pick up faint radio signals. It also helps to make sharp pictures which show us small objects.

Astronomers do not have to build vast radio telescopes. They can use a group of telescopes instead. This is called an **array**. The telescopes combine their signals. They work together as if they were one huge radio telescope. Radio telescopes around the world can be linked with **satellites** in space. Satellites are machines sent into orbit around the earth. Dishes linked up in this way are as powerful as one great radio telescope the size of the earth!

Looking for Life

A radio receiver can be used to turn radio waves into sound. The radio waves that come from space are not like the radio programs you hear on the radio. The only noise the waves make is a sort of hissing.

Each substance in space gives out radio waves of different wavelengths. If we measure wavelengths, we can find out which substances are in space. This is how we have found out that there is water in space. Water is made up of two gases, **hydrogen** and **oxygen**. Other things found in space contain a substance called **carbon** and a gas called **nitrogen**.

All these gases and substances are found in living things. You are made of them. Animals and plants are made of them. If these gases and substances exist in space, it could mean that there are other living things in the universe. They might be able to think and make things, or they might be like plants.

Space Messages

In the solar system, it seems likely that life exists only on the earth. When people landed on the moon, they found no life there. **Space probes** have visited other planets and moons. They have not found life in these places either.

How can we find out if there are living things far away in space? If they can think like we can, they might be sending out messages. These could be radio messages or light signals. We could send out signals from the earth to answer these messages and wait for a reply to come back from space.

26

Astronomers have used their radio telescopes to search for signals from space. So far, they have had no success in finding life.

Although we have not picked up any signals from space, there could still be life there. The galaxy is so huge that it takes radio waves and light rays many years to travel between the stars. A message could be on its way towards us now. It would take hundreds or even thousands of years to reach us. Sending a reply could take just as long. If other life exists, it is likely to be a very long way from the earth.

▶ The movie *ET* is about a being from a world far away in space. We do not know what another form of life would really look like.

▼ A message to the stars cannot be in English or any other human language. One way to send a message that other beings might understand is to use flashes of light or pulses of radio waves. The flashes or pulses can make up a simple code for numbers or pictures. Can you see what this message is saying? When arranged in a square, it shows a person's head.

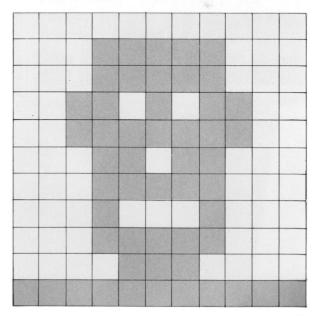

Above the Earth

When we watch the stars from the earth, we must look through the atmosphere. This layer of gases blocks off many rays from space. It also makes it harder for us to see light rays.

The best view of the stars is from space. In space there is no atmosphere to get in the way. Spacecraft can carry telescopes and other instruments into space. These instruments can send back signals and pictures to the earth.

Satellite Watch

Satellites are often used to watch the stars from space. Some are launched by rocket. Others can be put into orbit by the Space Shuttle.

▲ This satellite was launched in 1978. It was called the Einstein Observatory. Its job was to search for X-rays coming from outer space.

▼ Back on the earth, scientists look at pictures being sent back by the Einstein Observatory. The screens show X-rays coming from the Crab nebula.

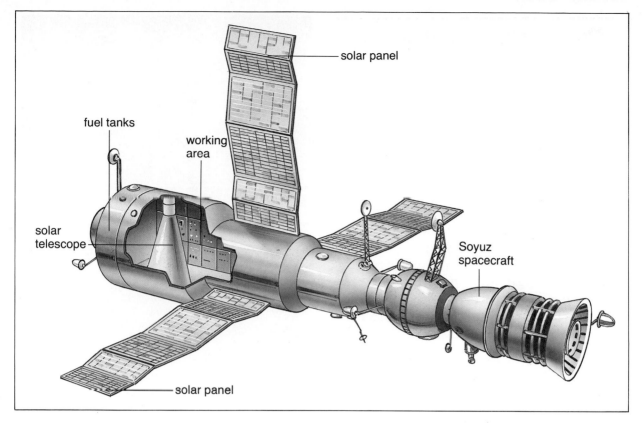

fuel tanks

working area

solar panel

solar telescope

Soyuz spacecraft

solar panel

People on the earth can control the satellites by radio. They can work the telescopes and cameras. They can pick up the stream of signals as they are sent back from space. Satellites can continue to work in space for months. Some remain in orbit for years.

Satellites are used to look at the sun, the stars, and the galaxies. They can pick up all kinds of rays, even the ones that do not reach the surface of the earth. They can measure objects in space. They can make measurements in space. The very first satellite was launched in 1957. It was called Sputnik 1. Since then, satellites have shown us all kinds of things that we would not have been able to see from the earth. We have learned a lot about black holes. Black holes suck in gas from space. As they do so, they send out X-rays. These have been picked up and their signals have been passed on to us by X-ray satellites.

▲ The USSR launched seven Salyut space stations in the 1970s and 1980s. Teams of astronauts flew up to the stations and back in Soyuz spacecraft.

People in Space

Some spacecraft have people on board. The people work the telescopes and other instruments. Some of these spacecraft are large **space stations**. They stay in orbit around the earth. Teams from the earth can visit the space stations. They can do all kinds of jobs. One thing they have done is to study the rays coming from the sun. They have helped us to find out how the sun works.

There are also **space laboratories**. These are launched into space for short lengths of time. Then, they return to the earth. Scientists can use these spacecraft as a workshop in space.

The Heat Seekers

You can feel rays from the sun as heat. You cannot see these rays. They can cross through space and they can also pass through air. The sun's heat reaches us over a distance of more than 93 million miles.

These heat rays are known as infrared rays. They are like light rays, but they have a longer wavelength. Special instruments can pick up the infrared rays that come from objects in space. They can make "heat" pictures of them. These pictures show which parts of an object are hotter or colder than others.

The Higher the Better

All objects in space send out infrared rays. By picking up these rays, we can find new objects. We can also learn new facts about objects we know already.

We use special kinds of reflecting telescopes to pick up these rays. The part of the telescope that forms the image has to be kept very cold. This helps it to detect very weak rays. The telescope has to be high up and in a dry place. This is because gas and drops of water in the air soak up infrared rays. One of the best sites is on the island of Hawaii in the Pacific Ocean. Some of the world's largest infrared telescopes have been built on top of the mountains there.

New Views of the Universe

Infrared telescopes and satellites have told us a great deal about the universe. We have found out that there are clouds of dust and gas around some stars. We cannot see them. Infrared telescopes can detect the clouds because they are warm. Planets may be forming inside the clouds. Learning

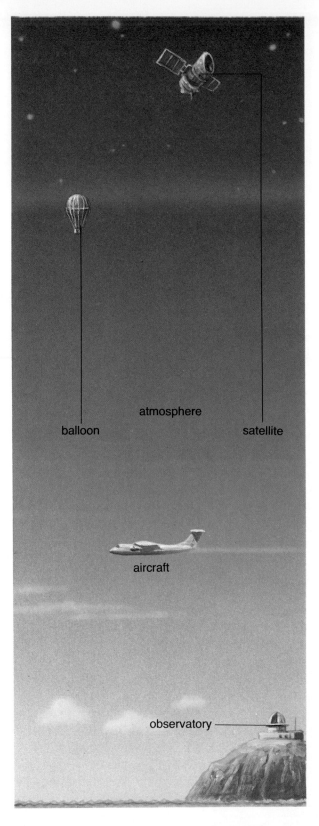

balloon

atmosphere

satellite

aircraft

observatory

about the clouds may explain how the earth and the solar system were first formed.

Infrared instruments can also be used to look through cool clouds of dust. They can show us the hot center of our galaxy. We now know that this is full of stars. Scientists think there may be a black hole at the center of our galaxy. Infrared telescopes may be able to solve this puzzle.

◄ Infrared telescopes must be very high up. Aircraft can carry them to four times the height of an observatory. Balloons can take them twice as high again. In space, infrared telescopes work a hundred times better.

► A model of IRAS, the Infrared Astronomy Satellite. It was launched in 1983. It mapped the sky for a year. It sent back pictures of about 250,000 infrared sources.

▼ An infrared picture of the Great Nebula in Orion. The source of the hottest rays has been colored white. Then come red, yellow, and green. The coldest sources are colored blue.

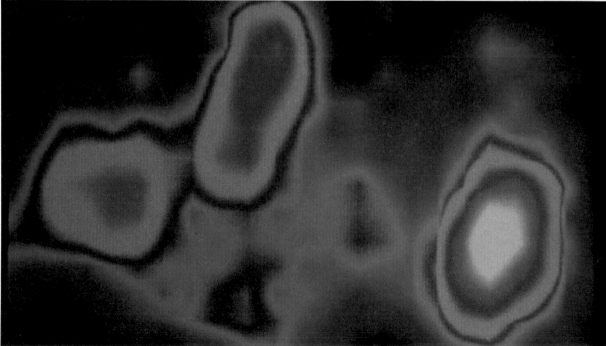

Other Kinds of Rays

The gases around the earth block off X-rays and gamma rays. This is good because these rays can harm living things. Most ultraviolet rays are blocked as well. A few ultraviolet rays are good for our health. They help our bodies make a substance called **vitamin D**. Balloons, rockets, and satellites are used to study all these rays.

Gamma Rays
Sources in space: Black holes, pulsars, quasars.
Space projects: In 1968, a satellite called OSO-3 was launched. It was the first to pick up gamma rays from beyond the solar system. A gamma ray observatory has been designed to be launched by the Space Shuttle.

▼ This is an X-ray picture taken by the Einstein Observatory. It shows the Virgo cluster of galaxies. There is a galaxy in the cluster called M87. It is a strong source of X-rays. This might be because a great black hole lies at the center of M87.

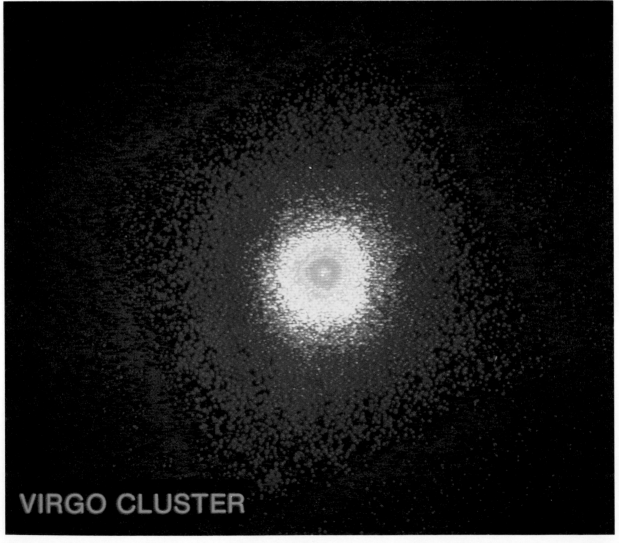

VIRGO CLUSTER

X-rays

Sources in space: Hot clouds of gas where new stars are being born. Pulsars and black holes.

Space projects: The Uhuru satellite was launched in 1970. It found a source of X-rays which was named Cygnus-1. This source puzzled people, for there was no star to be seen. We now think it is a black hole. It was the first one to be found. The Einstein Observatory was launched in 1978. It found X-rays coming from quasars. It recorded the wavelengths of the rays, and sent information back to the earth.

Ultraviolet rays

Sources in space: Very hot objects. Large and young stars.

Space projects: The Copernicus satellite was launched in 1972. It measured ultraviolet rays coming from the stars. The rays showed hydrogen that was made when the Universe first began. The International Ultraviolet Explorer was launched in 1978. It first found ultraviolet rays coming from galaxies.

▼ **The International Ultraviolet Explorer is a satellite with a telescope that detects ultraviolet rays. It has looked at very hot stars, and has helped us to find out how these stars burn.**

A Telescope in Space

The best telescope ever made is ready to begin work. It is waiting to be put into orbit 300 miles above the earth. It is called the Hubble **Space Telescope**, or HST for short. It is named after Edwin Hubble, a famous astronomer who discovered that the universe is growing bigger.

The HST picks up light rays just like optical telescopes on the earth. It is a reflecting telescope, forty-two feet long and fourteen feet wide. It weighs 12 tons. Out in space, it can work much better than the biggest telescopes on the ground. It can orbit above the layer of gases and dust that surrounds our planet.

The Power of the HST

The space telescope is able to show objects which are fifty times fainter than the faintest objects we can see now. It can show images ten times sharper than the best telescope on the earth. It is so powerful that it could see the face of a person 300 miles away. It is hoped that the HST will help us to find planets around nearby stars.

▶ After the HST has been launched by the Space Shuttle, it will orbit the earth. The solar panels on either side of the HST turn sunlight into electricity. This powers the telescope. Curved mirrors are used to reflect an image on to a microchip. This reacts to the light and makes electric signals. These are turned into radio signals by the HST. The radio signals are picked up by a satellite and beamed down to the the earth.

There are no people aboard the space telescope. The Shuttle can return to it if people have to look at it or repair it at any time. Every five years, the HST will be taken down to the earth for checking. It can then be launched again.

The HST can see seven times farther into the universe than any telescope that has been built before. It might find galaxies or other objects at the edge of the known universe. Their light will have taken 14 billion years to reach us. We would see the objects as they were long ago. We might be seeing them as they were at, or near, the beginning of the universe.

Probes to the Planets

▼ In 1985, the space probe Giotto was sent from the earth to look at Halley's comet. In 1986, it went through the comet's dusty tail. It looked at the center of the comet. It found that it was black and shaped like a peanut. It was nine miles long and five miles wide.

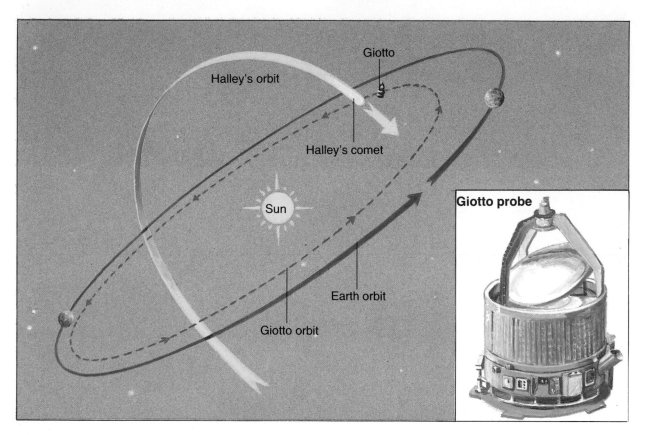

Giotto

Halley's orbit

Halley's comet

Sun

Earth orbit

Giotto orbit

Giotto probe

Several people flew to the moon between 1969 and 1972. They explored parts of the moon's surface. No one has yet flown to the planets in the solar system. Instead, space probes have visited the six planets nearest to us. Probes have landed on Mars and Venus. Other probes have looked at comets to see what they are like inside.

All space probes have cameras on board. They send pictures back to the earth by radio. We have seen detailed pictures of the surface of Mars and Venus. The pictures taken by space probes are far better than views seen through telescopes on the earth.

Exploring the Solar System

The first space probes explored the moon. In 1959, Luna 3 sent back a picture of the far side of the moon. We never see this side of the moon from the earth. This is because the moon spins just once in the time it takes to go round the earth. In 1966, Luna 9 landed on the moon and sent back pictures of the surface. Space probes to the moon showed that it was safe for people to go there.

Mariner 10 flew past the planet Mercury in 1974. Several Venera space probes have flown to Venus. Venera 9 sent back the first view of the surface of Venus in 1975.

Viking 1 was the first probe to land on Mars in 1976. The space probes showed that both Venus and Mars have a rocky surface.

One of the best space probes was Voyager 2. It flew past Jupiter in 1979 and Saturn in 1981. It passed Uranus in 1986. It sent back very clear views of the planets and their rings and moons.

Where Next?

Only two planets have not yet been explored by space probes. Voyager 2 is to fly past Neptune in August, 1989. There are at the moment no plans to visit Pluto, which is the farthest planet from the sun.

There are plans for further visits to some of the other planets. In 1988 or 1989, space probes are due to land on the two moons of Mars. In the 1990s, a space probe will study the atmosphere of Jupiter.

▼ The space probe Galileo has been made in order to fly to the planet Jupiter. It will orbit around the giant planet. It will send down instruments by parachute.

Robots in Space

A space probe has nobody on board to fly it. It is like a robot in space. A computer in the space probe controls the way it flies and works. The computer is told what to do before the probe leaves the earth. It can also be told to do things once it is in space. This is done by sending radio signals from the earth.

When the probe arrives at a planet, it may just fly past it, or it may go into orbit. It can take pictures of the planet and its moons or rings. A small part of the probe may leave the main part and land on the surface.

Getting Results

A space probe carries all kinds of instruments. The main one is a TV camera. Other instruments are used to pick up rays and measure them. If the probe lands on a planet, it can find out how hot it is on the surface. It may take a sample of the soil. It might even search for signs of life.

◀ The large dish of the Goldstone Tracking Station in California. It can send commands to space probes and get radio signals back. There are dishes like this around the world. They pick up signals as the earth spins around. Each one can stay in contact with the probe for a few hours each day.

All the instruments are electrical. The probe may get its electricity from **solar panels**. These panels turn sunlight into power. Solar panels cannot work far from the sun. Space probes have to use other ways of making electricity if they travel beyond Mars.

The facts and pictures gathered by the probe are turned into radio signals. The signals are sent back to the earth. The signals are very weak when they reach the earth. There, **ground stations** with huge radio dishes pick up the signals. Computers turn the signals back into pictures, and numbers.

▲ Io is one of the moons which go around the planet Jupiter. This picture was taken by a Voyager space probe. It flew past Jupiter in 1979. Io is covered with volcanoes.

◄ A Voyager space probe flies past the planet Saturn. It is taking pictures of the rings around the planet. It has all kinds of other instruments as well. The antenna beams the pictures back to the earth. They take over an hour to reach our planet.

The Big Bang

We have found out a lot about the universe. We have explored other planets in the solar system. We have looked at stars and distant galaxies. We have found pulsars and black holes. But we still have to solve the biggest puzzles of all. How big is the universe? How did it all begin? What will happen to it in the future?

The Growing Universe

We now know that each galaxy is moving at high speed. We can work out the speed when we measure its spectrum of light rays. We know that most of the galaxies are moving away from each other and that the universe is growing bigger all the time.

How long has the universe existed? Astronomers are not certain. They think that about fifteen billion years ago the universe was very small. It was crammed together in a tiny space. It may have been only the size of a golf ball!

The big crunch theory: the galaxies move apart after the big bang, but are then slowed down by the force of gravity. In the end, they stop, and gravity pulls the galaxies together again. Another big bang takes place, and a new universe is made. This idea is sometimes called the "closed universe."

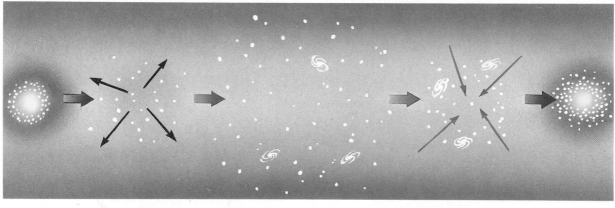

The big bang theory: the universe starts with a great explosion. The galaxies form and move away from each other. The force of gravity is too weak to pull the galaxies back together again. The universe continues to grow forever. This idea is sometimes known as the "open universe."

Then, some scientists think there was an explosion which we call the "big bang." The particles in the tiny universe all rushed apart. They formed gases and other substances, and these came together to make up galaxies of stars. The big bang was so huge that the galaxies have been moving apart ever since.

The Future

Will the universe continue to grow or will it stop? Perhaps, the galaxies will rush inwards again. They would all meet and crunch together in the middle. Then, there might be another big bang. A whole new universe would be made. Perhaps, this has happened before. Perhaps, the universe is always growing and shrinking.

Astronomers do not know the truth. They can only guess. It all depends on gravity. If there were enough stars and planets in the universe, then the force of all their gravity would be strong enough to pull the universe together again. The galaxies that we know about do not have enough force to do this on their own. It could be that there are dark parts of space that we cannot detect. These parts might stop the universe from growing. They might make it shrink and collapse.

▶ Albert Einstein was born in Germany in 1879. He later lived in Switzerland and the USA. Einstein was a scientist who changed our ideas of time and space. His ideas about gravity have helped us to understand black holes. Einstein also showed that nothing can travel faster than light. That is why people think that instant travel to the stars may be impossible.

Looking for Answers

Some astronomers do not spend all their time looking at stars. They find out what other astronomers have seen. They collect all the facts and study them. They then try to explain why the things they see happen as they do. They work out ideas, or **theories**. The idea that the universe started with a big bang is a theory. It is what people think might be true.

▼ An astronomer called Tycho Brahe lived in Denmark about 400 years ago. He measured the movements of the planets very carefully. Johann Kepler studied what Brahe had found out. He then worked out the way in which the planets move around the sun. This work took him many years.

Science works in this way. Facts are gathered and sorted. Theories are worked out. People must then find out if the theories are true.

Checking Out Ideas

Let us look at one theory. Astronomers think that the sun has a life of about ten billion years. It is now about halfway through its life. How have astronomers come to believe this?

They started by watching the sun. They measured it and found out how hot it is. They found out what makes the sun burn and which gases it is made of. They could then work out how fast the sun is burning up its gases. From these facts, they could guess how long the sun had been shining and when it would stop. The idea is still only a theory. New facts might be found out at any time. Then, the theory will have to be changed.

Astronomers look for ways in which a theory can be put to the test. They look for proof. Halley's comet is named after the astronomer Edmund Halley. He found out that the comet had been seen every 76 years for hundreds of years. He said it would appear again in 1758. When it did, his theory was proved to be right.

▼ The astronomer today can use computers to test any theories about the universe.

A computer can be used to check a theory. The computer is given all the known facts. It is then given a theory to check. It has to work out what would happen if the theory was right. In 1986, a computer was used to test a new theory about the moon. The theory said that the moon was made long ago when a planet crashed into the earth. The computer showed that if the crash had happened, the earth and moon would have been as they are today.

Into the Future

▶ The galaxy M81. Will a spacecraft ever reach the distant galaxies and travel through the universe?

▲ In 1975, an American Apollo spacecraft and a Russian Soyuz spacecraft linked up in space. Today, many countries work together in exploring space. Space must be used for the good of all the people on the earth.

What shall we find out about the universe next? It is full of surprises. We could find out something new at any moment.

In the 1990s, the HST and new satellites will look far into space. They could find stars that have planets. They may even find worlds like the earth. They may find out the true size of the universe. Perhaps, we shall solve the puzzle of how it all began and how it will all end.

Space probes will tell us more about the other planets of the solar system. People may travel to some of them, too. A possible visit to Mars is being planned. We may begin to explore the universe beyond the solar system. We may send probes to the nearby stars.

Science Facts

The stars are very far away. It would take many thousands of years for people to fly there in the kind of spacecraft we have now. We have all seen films about the future. Could they really become true? Could a spacecraft travel to the stars in a flash?

Scientists know no way of making these things happen. Maybe they never will. If people do fly to the stars, they may have to live on board their spacecraft for hundreds of years. People may live and die in space.

Hundreds of years ago, people set out in small boats to explore the earth. Today, we are setting out on an even greater journey. We are going to explore the universe.

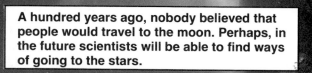

A hundred years ago, nobody believed that people would travel to the moon. Perhaps, in the future scientists will be able to find ways of going to the stars.

Glossary

antenna: the part of a radio dish which can pick up radio signals, or send them out.

array: a number of objects or instruments laid out so they can be seen easily.

astronomer: someone who studies the stars and planets and other objects in space.

astronomy: the study of the stars and planets and other objects in space.

atmosphere: the layer of gases which surrounds a planet or star. The earth's atmosphere is the air.

binoculars: a kind of double telescope with two eyepieces.

black hole: the remains of a star. It has very strong gravity. It sucks in every object that is around it in space. It even pulls back rays of light. This is why we cannot see a black hole with our eyes.

calendar: a list or table showing all the days, dates, and months of the year.

carbon: one of the substances found in all living things on the earth.

cluster: a group of galaxies.

comet: a ball of frozen gas and dust which travels around the sun.

constellation: a group of stars as it is seen from the earth.

cosmic ray: a tiny piece of matter which streams out from the sun through space.

dome: a rounded roof. It is shaped like half an orange.

dust: tiny pieces of solid matter. A lot of dust floats around in space.

electricity: a kind of energy or power which can travel along wires. It is used to make heat and light and to work machines.

electronic: able to store and use electrical signals. A computer is electronic.

elliptical: shaped like an egg or a squashed circle. The paths followed by planets around the sun are elliptical.

false-color image: colors used to show different parts of a picture. They are not the real colors of the object shown.

filter: a piece of colored glass. It can be placed in front of a camera so that it blocks off certain colors.

galaxy: a very large group of stars, planets, dust, and gases which are all loosely held together by gravity. Together, the galaxies make up the universe. Our own galaxy is called the Milky Way.

gamma ray: one of a group of rays which has the shortest wavelength of all.

gas: a substance that is neither liquid nor solid. Air is made up of several gases.

gravity: the force that pulls objects towards each other. The earth's gravity keeps us on the earth. Gravity makes things fall and gives them weight.

ground station: a place where radio signals from satellites can be picked up.

hydrogen: the lightest substance in the universe. The sun is made of hydrogen gas.

infrared: rays which are longer than red light waves we can see. We feel them as heat.

instrument: a tool made by people to help them to do something. A telescope is an instrument which helps us see a long way.

interferometer: a device used to measure wavelengths.

lens: a piece of glass that is curved to focus light. Lenses are used in telescopes, binoculars, and cameras.

microchip: a tiny piece of silicon which is used to carry electricity.

moon: a smaller body that orbits a planet. Jupiter has sixteen moons. The earth has only one moon. The moon has no atmosphere and no life.

nebula: a cloud of gas and dust in space.

nitrogen: a gas found in all living things and many parts of the universe. It has no color, smell, or taste. It does not burn.

observatory: a building or spacecraft from which astronomers watch the skies.

optical telescope: an instrument which uses lenses and mirrors. It picks up light rays so that we can see distant objects more clearly.

orbit: the path through space made by one thing going around another. The earth is in orbit around the sun.

oxygen: the gas found in air and water. Oxygen is very important to all plants and animals. We cannot breathe without oxygen.

particle: a tiny speck of solid matter.

photon counter: a device which can be fixed to a telescope. It can record a tiny amount of light and make it brighter.

planet: a body in space which moves around a star like the sun. The planet shines by reflecting the light of the star. It can be made of rock, metal, or gas.

prism: a piece of glass shaped like a triangle which breaks up light into the colors of the rainbow.

pulsar: the remains of a dead star which gives off a regular pulse of light or radio waves as it spins.

quasar: an object far away in space which looks like a star. It sends out far more light or other rays than a star.

radio dish: a dish-shaped bowl on a radio telescope or spacecraft. It collects and sends out radio waves and signals.

radio telescope: a telescope that picks up radio waves instead of light.

radio wave: a ray which has the longest wavelength of all, from a fraction of an inch to many miles.

reflect: to throw back heat, light, or sound from a surface.

reflecting telescope: a kind of telescope which works with mirrors.

refracting telescope: a kind of telescope which works with a lens.

satellite: a small body in orbit around a larger body in space. The moon is a satellite of the earth. We also call spacecraft that orbit the earth satellites.

Schmidt telescope: a telescope which can take photographs of a very large area of the sky at one time.

silicon: a common substance found in the earth's rocks.

solar panel: a large, flat area, or panel, that easily absorbs heat from the sun.

solar system: the sun and all the objects that orbit it, such as planets and moons.

space: the area between the planets and the stars. Space is almost empty. It contains tiny amounts of gas and dust.

spacecraft: any vehicle which travels into space.

space laboratory: a spacecraft where scientific tests can be carried out in space.

space probe: a machine sent from the earth to study parts of the solar system. It does not have people on board.

space station: a large spacecraft that stays in orbit around the earth. It is big enough for people to live and work on board.

space telescope: a large telescope that stays in space. It is put into orbit around the earth.

spectrograph: a machine which measures the spectrum of light given off by a star or other object.

spectrum: a range. The complete spectrum of radiation includes gamma rays, X rays, ultraviolet, light, infrared, and radio waves. The spectrum of light we can see is made up of the colors of the rainbow.

star: a glowing ball of gas that gives off its own heat and light. The sun is a star.

sun: the star nearest to the earth. It gives us all our heat and light.

sundial: a simple device for telling time from a shadow cast by the sun.

telescope: an instrument that you look through to make distant objects, such as the moon, appear bigger. **Never point a telescope at the sun. You will damage your eyes.**

theory: an idea about something that is not yet known to be a fact.

ultraviolet: rays which have a shorter wavelength than the blue light we can see.

universe: all of space and everything in it.

vitamin D: a substance which makes your teeth and bones strong. It is found in milk and some foods. Some ultraviolet rays help make vitamin D.

wavelength: the distance between the top of one wave and the top of the next. It is how we measure different kinds of rays, such as light, which travel in a wavy motion.

X-rays: rays with a wavelength shorter than ultraviolet and longer than gamma rays. They are given out by super-hot gases in space.